DR JEKYLL AND MR HYDE

化身博士

原著/[英]罗伯特·路易斯·史蒂文森

改编 / [英]彼德·克罗瑟

插图 / [英]瓦妮莎·卢巴赫

REAL READS

中央广播电视大学出版社·北京

图书在版编目（CIP）数据

化身博士／（英）罗伯特·路易斯·史蒂文森原著；（英）彼德·克罗瑟改编；（英）瓦妮莎·卢巴赫插图．—北京：中央广播电视大学出版社，2016.12

ISBN 978－7－304－08089－1

Ⅰ.①化… Ⅱ.①罗… ②彼… ③瓦… Ⅲ.①英语—语言读物 ②长篇小说—英国—近代 Ⅳ.①H319.4：I

中国版本图书馆 CIP 数据核字（2016）第 253806 号

图字：01－2013－5463

化身博士
HUASHEN BOSHI
［英］罗伯特·路易斯·史蒂文森 原著
［英］彼德·克罗瑟 改编 ［英］瓦妮莎·卢巴赫 插图

出版·发行：中央广播电视大学出版社
电话：营销中心 010－66490011 总编室 010－68182524
网址：http://www.crtvup.com.cn
地址：北京市海淀区西四环中路 45 号 **邮编：**100039
经销：新华书店北京发行所

策划统筹：郑 毅 **责任编辑：**李 刚 **策划编辑：**李 刚 朱亚宁
责任印制：赵连生 **责任校对：**赵 洋

印刷：北京中科印刷有限公司
版本：2016 年 12 月第 1 版 2016 年 12 月第 1 次印刷
开本：130mm×187mm **印张：**3.875 **字数：**67 千字

书号：ISBN 978－7－304－08089－1
定价：28.00 元

（如有缺页或倒装，本社负责退换）

前　言

人大附中英语组　杨乐硕士

罗伯特·路易斯·史蒂文森（Robert Louis Stevenson，1850—1894），出生于英国苏格兰的全才作家，从小就体弱多病，日后更患上结核病。虽于二十五岁取得律师资格，但他一向对法律兴味索然，而且当时他已开始从事写作，是以终其一生从未担任过一天真正的执业律师。

1883年出版的《金银岛》（Treasure Island）让史蒂文森声名大噪，这是他首部长篇小说作品；1886年的《化身博士》（The Strange Case of Dr. Jekyll and Mr. Hyde）和《绑架》（Kidnapped），一推出即跃升为最畅销书籍，更奠定了他屹立不摇的作家地位。他曾游历欧洲各国及美国等地，且于1876年在法国邂逅了年长他十岁的美籍妻子，而这些游历见闻也成为他创作旅行游记以及《金银岛》一书的素材。

这位长年受结核病折磨的伟大作家，最终于1894年与朋友在家聚会时，意外地因脑溢血而与世长辞，当时他才正值四十四岁的英年。

《化身博士》

杰科尔博士研制出了一种药剂，在他每晚喝下这种药剂后，便会化身为邪恶的海德先生四处作恶，他终日徘徊在善恶之间，其内心的良知和犯罪的快感不断冲突，令他饱受折磨，直至完全崩溃。这种貌似荒诞无稽的故事，其实蕴含了最深刻的人性命题：人的本性究竟是善是恶？是如同一枚硬币的两面那样黑白分明，还是亦正亦邪，时善时恶？《化身博士》是史蒂文森的得意之作，因为书中人物杰科尔和海德截然不同的性格让人印象深刻，后来“Jekyll and Hyde”一词竟成为心理学“双重人格”的代称。根据这部作品改编的还有同名音乐剧和电影等。

科幻小说阅读与英语学习

科学幻想小说（Science Fiction）简称科幻小说，主要描写想象的科学或技术对社会或个人的影响的虚构性文学作品。科幻小说是西方近代文学的一种新体裁。它的情节不可能发生在人们已知的世界中，但它的基础是有关人类或宇宙起源的某种设想，或是有关科技领域（包括假设性的科技领域）某种虚构出来的新发现。在当代的西方世界，科幻小说因其大胆的想象，带给了人们新奇、刺激的阅读体验，并成为了广受欢迎的通俗读物。

英语长篇小说的阅读不仅可以帮助读者积

累大量原汁原味的英语表达方式，同时对于提高文章理解力以及写作能力也很有帮助，使读者能更加有效地驾驭英语阅读，快速把握关键信息并在英语写作中更有逻辑性，同时富有感染力。此外，科幻小说独有的将科学想象转化为语言叙事的写作风格亦能提高读者对于科技领域事件的叙述能力。

科幻小说与人文思辨

科幻小说充满了对于科学的论辩或是理论叙述，在阅读之前，我们可能对于这些科学概念充满幻想，然而在阅读的过程中我们又会在作者的带领下不断挑战并修正这些幻想与观点。例如在《科学怪人》中，我们一开始赞叹科学的成就，可以创造出一个新的人类，但是后来这个新人类却因为无法融入现有的人类社会变成了一个暴力怪物，同时这个怪物在犯下各种罪行后还会为自己辩解。我们到底是该同情他还是该谴责他呢？我们不禁开始怀疑科学创造智慧生物的神话是否可行，如果可行的话，我们又会面临哪些道德问题，该如何处理？人类目前掌握的克隆技术以及机器人的开发是否应受到严格的控制呢？这一连串的科技与人类如何共处的争议话题引领读者进入了一个思辨的世界。在阅读科幻小说的过程中，读者一方面可以体验科技发展的巨大潜力，开发想象力，另一方面也可以思考科技发展对人类社会的影响，提高人文素养。

CONTENTS

请扫描此二维码下载“开放云书院”App，即可在线收听本书配套音频，领略正宗英式英语的魅力。

THE CHARACTERS

Dr Henry Jekyll

Can this respectable doctor resist the strange powers of Mr Hyde?

Edward Hyde

Who is this man and what is the mysterious hold he has over Dr Jekyll?

Mr Utterson

Mr Utterson is Dr Jekyll's friend and lawyer. Can he solve the mystery? Can he save his friend?

Richard Enfield

What information does Richard Enfield possess? Will he save or condemn Dr Jekyll?

Poole

Poole is Dr Jekyll's faithful butler. Can he save his master from himself?

Dr Hastie Lanyon

Dr Lanyon witnesses a terrifyingly strange event. How will he react?

Inspector Newcomen

Inspector Newcomen is one of Scotland Yard's finest. Can he discover Edward Hyde's true identity, and solve a brutal murder?

• butler (n.) 男管家

DR JEKYLL AND MR HYDE

♪01 'You know,' Enfield said to his friend Utterson the lawyer as they strolled through a down-at-heel part of London, 'that house over there is etched in my mind in connection with a strange story.'

'Indeed?' Utterson remarked, looking at the sinister block of buildings at which his friend was pointing. 'Do tell.'

'I was coming home late, about three o'clock of a black winter morning, and my way lay through this part of town. Just here, where we are standing, I saw the oddest thing. Some fellow trampled calmly all over a young girl, then left her screaming on the ground.'

'Whatever for?'

Enfield shook his head. 'No reason, save that she ran into him by accident.'

'So the girl's fault, then?'

- etch (v.) 深印
- sinister (a.) 不祥的
- trample (v.) 踩，践踏

'Perhaps. But the man—a singularly distasteful fellow to be sure—made to walk off, until I collared him and then called a doctor to the scene to attend the child.'

'Was the fellow drunk?'

'Not to my knowledge. A crowd built up baying for his blood, but the doctor and I held them off.'

'And this house,' Utterson said, 'how is it relevant?'

'Under threat of a lawsuit on the part of the girl's parents— which would surely have been successful—we managed to persuade him to pay one hundred pounds as compensation for his behaviour. At first the fellow was reluctant, but I think he feared the

- singularly (adv.) 非常地
- distasteful (a.) 使人不愉快的，讨厌的
- collar (v.) 抓住……的领口
- attend (v.) 照料，护理

crowd, and finally he led us to this very dwelling, disappeared inside, and returned with ten pounds in coin and a cheque for the balance.'

'Hmph!' Utterson snorted. 'I'll wager the cheque was—'

'No,' Enfield interrupted. 'I was wary myself, but we all repaired to my rooms until the bank opened later that day. When we went down to the bank they confirmed that the cheque was genuine, and the family got their ninety pounds.'

'And that was the end of it?'

Enfield shrugged and nodded, and the pair started to walk again.

'What was the fellow's name?'

'Hyde,' Enfield replied, his voice little more than a whisper. 'Edward Hyde. But that wasn't the name on the cheque.'

Utterson stopped again. 'Edward Hyde, you say?'

Enfield nodded. 'Whatever is the matter, my dear Utterson?'

- dwelling (n.) 住宅
- snort (v.) 喷鼻息
- wager (v.) 同……打赌
- wary (a.) 小心翼翼的，警惕的
- repair (v.) 聚集

'Nothing, my dear chap. I thought for a moment I knew the fellow—or knew of him.'

As they passed by a jetty where a young boy sat, his line cast out into the murky water, Enfield said, 'You didn't ask me the name on the bounder's cheque.'

Utterson nodded, smiling grimly, and, after a few seconds, he said, 'That is because I believe I know it already.' What he did not say was that he knew the owner of the house whose rear entrance was the very door that Enfield had pointed out.

♪02 Back at his own house, Utterson lost no time in retrieving some documents from his safe. He leafed through them until he found an envelope bearing the words 'Dr Henry Jekyll's Will'. He

- chap (n.) 家伙，男人(口语)
- jetty (n.) 防波堤
- murky (a.) 黑暗的
- bounder (n.) 粗鲁的人
- retrieve (v.) 取回
- leaf (v.) 翻阅

opened the envelope and, by the flickering light of a candle, he discovered the sentence he sought: in the event of Jekyll's death, all possessions were to pass into the hands of the doctor's 'friend and benefactor' Edward Hyde. Moreover, the document continued, if the doctor were to disappear for a time exceeding three months, Hyde should step fully into Henry Jekyll's shoes. He would be free of any financial obligations save the payment of a few small sums to the doctor's household.

'I have no idea what might be going on, nor what hold this Hyde fellow might have on you, Henry Jekyll,' Utterson whispered to the room, 'but I swear I will make it my business to find out.'

♪03 For the next few days, Utterson did make it his business to spend as much time as possible in the vicinity of the building his friend Enfield

• benefactor (n.) 捐助人，恩人 • vicinity (n.) 附近地区

had pointed out. If he be Mr Hyde, he thought, I shall be Mr Seek.

One evening, at a little after ten o'clock, his patience was finally rewarded. He heard footsteps echoing down the street. Utterson withdrew into a shop doorway and waited. A man appeared out of the gloom into the small pool of gaslight, reached into his pocket, and produced a key. He was small—almost stunted—and plainly dressed, his face shrouded by the brim of his hat. Although he glanced furtively from side to side, he failed to spot Utterson until he was across the street and almost at the door to the house.

'Mr Hyde, I think?' Utterson said softly as he stepped out of the shadows.

- gloom (n.) 暗处
- produce (v.) 拿出
- stunt (v.) 阻碍……的发育
- shroud (v.) 覆盖
- furtively (adv.) 偷偷地

The man shrank back with a sharp intake of breath, still managing to keep his face hidden. 'What do you want?' he asked, his voice harsh.

Utterson nodded to the door of the house. 'I'm a friend of Dr Jekyll. I thought we might talk inside.'

'Who are you?'

'Utterson of Gaunt Street,' said Utterson. 'You must surely have heard my name.' As Hyde shook his head, Utterson continued. 'I thought you might admit me.'

'You will not find Dr Jekyll here; he is away from home. How do you know me?'

Utterson did not answer that question, instead asking another. 'Will you do me a favour?'

'What is it?' asked Hyde suspiciously.

'Will you let me see your face?' asked the lawyer.

Edward Hyde hesitated, and then, as if suddenly changing his mind, looked straight at Utterson with an air of defiance. In the

- intake (n.) 吸收
- harsh (a.) 严厉的
- admit (v.) 准许进入
- defiance (n.) 反抗

lamplight, Utterson noticed how Hyde's brows met in thick black hair and his face was pale, the eyes glinting like those of a fish—barely human, in fact.

'Now I shall recognise you again,' said Utterson. 'It may be useful.'

'Yes,' returned Hyde, 'perhaps it is as well we have met. I think you should also have my address,' and he gave the lawyer a number of a street in Soho. Good god, thought Utterson, is he thinking that I shall need his address in order to fulfil the terms of Dr Jekyll's will?

'Now you shall tell me how you know me,' said Hyde.

'We have friends in common,' Utterson said. 'Dr Jekyll, for a start.'

Hyde's eyes flashed wide. 'What has Jekyll told you about me?' he cried, with a flush of anger. Without waiting for an answer, Hyde unlocked

• glint (v.) 闪烁

the door and disappeared into the house.

What on earth could possibly link Jekyll with such an unpleasant man, Utterson wondered. One thing was certain—whatever it was, such a link could only be bad for the doctor. He decided that there was only one course left open to him. He must talk to Henry Jekyll.

♪04 Round the corner from the sinister building where Hyde had disappeared there was a square of ancient, handsome houses, going somewhat to seed. One house still wore a great air of wealth and comfort, though it was now in darkness except for the fan-light. At the door of this house Mr Utterson stopped and knocked.

Presently, Jekyll's elderly butler—slightly stooped but with sharp clear eyes—pulled open the door. His face immediately broke into

- fan-light (n.) 扇形窗，天窗
- stoop (v.) 屈身，弯腰

a broad smile.

'Oh, Mr Utterson, sir,' the man said cheerfully. 'I fear the master is away from home.'

Utterson nodded regretfully. 'No matter, Poole. I shall see him another time.' Then he said, 'I believe I saw Mr Hyde come in by the old dissecting room door earlier. Is that right, with the doctor away?'

'Quite right, sir. The gentleman has a key.'

'Your master seems to have placed a great deal of trust in this fellow,' he observed as he moved back onto the step.

'Yes sir,' Poole agreed. 'We all of us have orders to obey him, though he never dines here. In fact, we see very little of him on this side of the house. He mostly comes and goes through the laboratory.'

On the way home through the fog, Utterson's mind whirled. He was glad when he reached the familiarity of his own front door and went inside.

- dissect (v.) 解剖
- whirl (v.) 头晕眼花，感到混乱

♪05 'I have been wanting to speak with you, Henry,' Utterson said. He had stayed behind for a final drink after one of Dr Jekyll's famous dinner parties.

'With regard to what, my dear friend?'

'Your will,' came the reply.

Jekyll snorted. 'My will?'

'Yes. It's Hyde. I have been hearing something of the fellow.'

Jekyll got to his feet. 'I do not care to hear more.'

'But what I heard was—'

Jekyll waved a hand. 'No. You do not understand my position. I am somewhat ... somewhat painfully situated. In brief, my position in this matter is very strange. I know you have seen him,' Jekyll continued. 'He told me so. And I fear he was rude to you. Nevertheless, I want you to promise that, in the event that I am taken away, you will look after him and his rights.'

Utterson saw the folly of arguing: his friend's mind was made up. 'I can't pretend that I shall ever like him,' he said softly.

'I do not ask for that. I ask only for justice.'

'Very well,' Utterson said at last. 'I promise.'

♪06 Jekyll watched his friend disappear up the street before checking that the outer door was locked. Then he told Poole that he did not want to be disturbed and retired into his laboratory.

There, amidst bubbling pipettes and flasks, the doctor pulled from the shelves a small array of vials, the liquids from which he began to mix together carefully in a glass. When he was satisfied with the

- pipet (n.) 量管
- flask (n.) 烧瓶
- vial (n.) 小玻璃瓶

result, he lifted the glass to his mouth and, with a momentary pause, tilted it back and swallowed the whole mixture.

Almost immediately he slumped against the heavy wooden counter, his face a mask of pain. Eyes tightly shut and mouth clenched, he clutched his stomach and folded over, stifling a deep moan. Even as he bent forward, his body was already thickening, changing—sinew, muscle, artery, all of them expanding or contracting. Churning noises rumbled from his stomach, cartilage and bone twanged and cracked as his neck grew shorter and his neatly-styled hair exploded into a dense thatch.

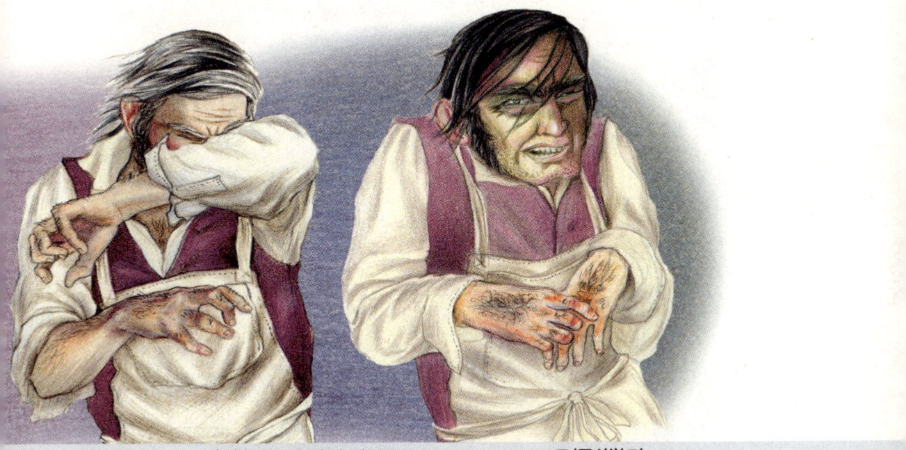

- slump (v.) (突然或沉重地)倒下
- clench (v.) 咬紧
- stifle (v.) 抑制
- sinew (n.) 腱
- artery (n.) 动脉
- churn (v.) 剧烈搅动
- rumble (v.) 隆隆响
- cartilage (n.) 软骨
- twang (v.) 发出“砰”的一声
- thatch (n.) 茅草

In those brief seconds while the change was under way, Henry Jekyll was flooded with regret. But then, when the change was complete, there were no such reservations. It was like an easing of pain, his long-held everyday identity, with all of its restrictions, fell away from him and left in its place a profound alertness unfettered by the constraints and sensibilities imposed by society. He felt a smile take his mouth and spread it wide.

Henry Jekyll, respected doctor and gentleman of the parish, was now Edward Hyde. The world and all its untamed pleasures belonged to him.

- flood (v.) 充满
- reservation (n.) 异议
- unfetter (v.) 使自由，从束缚中解放出来

He changed his clothes for some more suited to his radically altered shape and, making sure he did not wake Poole, he slipped out into the night.

07 Utterson had made a very emphatic promise to his friend, and saw no reason to continue his pursuit of Edward Hyde. Over the following months he threw his energy into his work.

Utterson saw Jekyll from time to time, though perhaps not as often as they had both once enjoyed. Jekyll explained that he was very busy with his work, and the time-consuming research about which he would never speak.

What Jekyll did not tell Utterson, however, was that he was able to continue taking the miraculous potion without any serious consequences, thus living a double life.

• emphatic (a.) 有力的

But what had started as a brave scientific experiment soon became a lunatic addiction. As his metabolism grew accustomed to the effects of the mixture, and his temperament became more comfortable as Mr Hyde, Dr Jekyll had to increase the dosage of the antidote each time he wanted to return to his more responsible self. However, he could not have foreseen the dreadful event that would change everything.

♪08 About a year after Utterson had spoken to Dr Jekyll about his friend Hyde, London was startled by a crime of singular ferocity. The details were few and startling. A maidservant, living alone in a house not far from the river, had gone upstairs to bed about eleven. When she glanced out of the window she saw a scruffy and heavy-set man encounter a well-dressed gentleman taking an evening stroll.

- lunatic (a.) 疯狂的
- metabolism (n.) 新陈代谢
- dosage (n.) 剂量
- singular (a.) 奇特的
- ferocity (n.) 残暴的行为
- scruffy (a.) 不整齐的，肮脏的
- heavy-set (a.) 体格魁梧的

She immediately recognised the scruffy man as Edward Hyde who had, on occasion, visited her master. She saw the smarter gentleman raise his hat. Although she could not hear what was said, she assumed that it was polite conversation. She was therefore astonished to see Hyde suddenly enraged. Sweeping his walking-stick like a sabre, he attacked the other man, showing not an ounce of mercy.

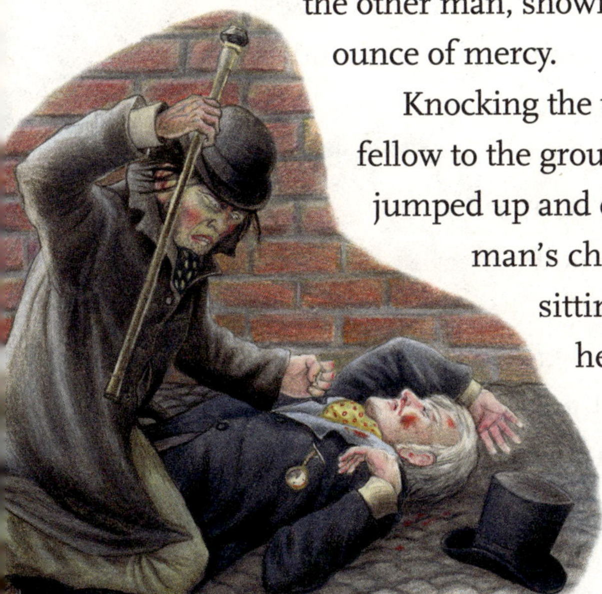

Knocking the unfortunate fellow to the ground, Hyde jumped up and down on the man's chest. Finally, sitting astride him, he beat his head to a pulp.

The maid, having

- sabre (n.) 军刀
- astride (adv.) 跨着
- pulp (n.) 黏浆状物质

seen the whole thing, was able to give the police both a description of the attacker and his name. At the scene of the crime, a constable found part of a walking stick, still bloodied. In one of the unidentifiable victim's pockets was a stamped envelope with Utterson's name on it. When the police visited Utterson, the lawyer asked to see the body.

'It is as I feared,' Utterson said, his words heavy with regret. 'It is my very good friend Sir Danvers Carew.' He nodded to the morgue attendant, who covered the body. 'If you come with me in my cab,' he said to the senior policeman, 'I can take you to the murderer's house.' And he led the way to a certain address in Soho.

• constable (n.) 警察

• morgue (n.) 停尸间

♪09 A dishevelled old woman answered the door. 'Oh,' she said with a hoarse and throaty chuckle. ''E's not 'ere.' She seemed reluctant to let the men into the house, but when Inspector Newcomen of Scotland Yard stepped forward she relented. In fact, she seemed quietly delighted at the possibility that her master had fallen foul of the law.

Hyde's rooms were a mess, with clothes lying in heaps and pockets turned inside out as though a burglary had taken place.

- dishevelled (a.) 不整的，凌乱的
- hoarse (a.) 粗哑的
- throaty (a.) 低沉的
- chuckle (n.) 咕咕声
- relent (v.) 变温和

But amidst the chaos they found the other half of the walking stick and, in the fireplace, a partly burned chequebook. A visit to Hyde's bank showed there to be several thousand pounds in the man's account.

That afternoon Utterson paid a visit to the home of Henry Jekyll, and expressed the hope that the doctor was not harbouring the murderer.

'I most certainly am not,' Jekyll told his friend. Then, with seeming embarrassment he added, 'And I can assure you that the man will not be heard from again.'

To support this intention, Jekyll produced a letter he had received that very day. The letter, from Hyde, was written in an almost childlike and barely intelligible scrawl. In a few brief lines, the missive's author thanked Jekyll for his support, and explained that he had the means to escape the city. Jekyll would not hear from him again.

- harbour (v.) 庇护
- intelligible (a.) 可理解的，清晰的
- scrawl (n.) 潦草模糊的笔迹
- missive (n.) 书信

Utterson was relieved by all of this, but nevertheless enquired as to the envelope in which Hyde's letter had arrived. Jekyll became quite defensive. 'Why, I burned it,' he exclaimed, 'but it would have offered no clue as to the fellow's whereabouts.'

'The envelope would surely have had a postal mark?' The doctor shook his head emphatically. 'It was delivered by hand.'

'I wonder, might I borrow this?'

'His letter? Of course, by all means—take the blessed thing away.'

'And now one word more: it was Hyde who dictated the terms in your will about that disappearance?' Utterson asked. The doctor seemed seized with a qualm of faintness: he shut his mouth tight and nodded.

'I knew it,' said Utterson. 'He meant to murder you. You have had a fine escape.'

'I have had what is far more to the purpose,' returned the doctor solemnly: 'I have had a lesson,

- dictate (v.) 要求
- qualm (n.) 不适

Utterson. What a lesson I have had!' He covered his face for a moment with his hands.

As Utterson donned his coat and hat, Jekyll became more cheerful.

'On a happier note, I would like to know if you can dine with me later in the month.'

Utterson was pleased to accept, and the doctor promised to send a formal invitation to remind his friend of the arrangement and the date.

On the way out, Utterson asked Poole what the messenger was like who had delivered Hyde's envelope.

'Messenger, Mr Utterson? There has been no messenger here today.'

'Are you sure, Poole?'

'Quite sure, sir.'

• don (v.) 穿上，披上

♪10 Back in his offices, Utterson recounted the afternoon's events to his chief clerk, Mr Guest, who suggested that Hyde must be mad. Utterson showed Guest Hyde's letter.

'No, perhaps not mad; but it is certainly exceedingly odd handwriting.'

At that very moment, Utterson's manservant brought a note to his master. It was Dr Jekyll's invitation to dinner and, catching sight of it, Guest asked to see it. The manservant handed the note across and Guest placed it on the desk alongside Hyde's letter. His face a mask of incredulity, he turned to Utterson. Guest shuffled the two letters around for Utterson to see. 'It is clear to me, Mr Utterson, that, despite some obvious and marked differences between the two hands, there are distinct similarities.'

'Similarities?' Utterson leaned forward and glanced first at the familiar copperplate script of his friend Henry Jekyll, and then at the

- recount (v.) 叙述
- incredulity (n.) 不相信，怀疑
- shuffle (v.) 把……移来移去
- copperplate (a.) 工整的

uneven childlike—or perhaps even drunken—scrawl of Edward Hyde. 'I fear I simply do not see any resemblance between the two hands.'

Guest overlapped the two notes and pointed out certain elements—the curlicued script ending of words finishing in the letters 'ing', the very specific placing of the dot above the letter 'i' in both instances, the somewhat flamboyant bar on capital versions of the letters 'A' and 'H'.

'My goodness,' was all that Utterson could bring himself to say. Did this mean that his friend had forged a note for a murderer? He placed the letter purporting to be from Edward Hyde in his safe, and retired to his rooms for the evening.

- curlicue (n.)(书法) 花体
- flamboyant (a.) 浮夸的
- purport (v.) 号称

11 A reward was immediately offered for information leading to Hyde's arrest, but no such information was forthcoming.

The days turned into weeks and the weeks into months. During this time, Dr Jekyll regained much of his previous heartiness and health, renewing his acquaintance with friends upon whom he had turned his back.

Behind the facade, however, the temptation to become Hyde again, to live beyond the restraints of civil society, whispered in his head. Whenever he looked into a mirror he seemed to see the gnarled countenance of Edward Hyde leering at him, prodding him onwards to concoct a new batch of the wicked serum.

At last the doctor succumbed—and it was a different man entirely from the staid Dr Jekyll who crept out of the house into London's mist-filled, cobbled alleyways.

- facade (n.) 表面
- gnarled (a.)(手、指) 粗糙的
- leer (v.) 斜着眼看
- prod (v.) 刺激
- concoct (v.) 图谋，策划
- serum (n.) 浆液
- succumb (v.) 屈服
- staid (a.) 稳重的
- cobbled (a.) 铺有大卵石的

Some time later, on this fateful evening, Edward Hyde spotted a man travelling home from a hostelry. He waited for the man behind a wall and then leapt out into his path.

'Good evening,' Hyde said.

As the man frowned, Hyde brought his cane across the fellow's head, hitting him a further three times even as the man was slumping to the ground in a bloody heap.

• hostelry (n.) 旅店

• cane (n.) 手杖

Without so much as a second's consideration, Hyde removed the man's wallet and, with a final two-handed swing of the cane into the lifeless man's face, hurried off into the night.

♪12 Safe once more in Jekyll's laboratory, Hyde prepared some more potion and drank it down, collapsing to the floor amidst broken glass. When he came to, he was the doctor once again. 'Oh god,' he sobbed, his hands clasped together as if in prayer, 'help me to stop this thing that is happening to me.'

• potion (n.) 一剂

For a few days, Jekyll was able to control the urge to mix more of the potion. Though it was hard, his life slowly regained some of its former normality and he stayed around the house, splitting his time between his surgeries, his meals alone and his beloved books.

Then, one night, he dreamed a strange dream. In the dream, his skin crawled as though beset by the maggots he used in his surgery to clean post-operative wounds. He could feel them moving around on his arms and legs, on his neck and his face, but somehow it felt as though they were actually inside him. He sat up with a start, his eyes wide open, and he glanced nervously around the moonlit room. What had awakened him so abruptly?

As soon as the thought had formed, a fierce abdominal pain caused him to bend over. Only a grim determination prevented him from crying out, for he did not want to bring Poole rushing to his bedroom.

- crawl (v.) 爬满，充斥着
- beset (v.) 包围住
- maggot (n.) 蛆
- abdominal (a.) 腹部的
- grim (a.) 坚强的，不屈的

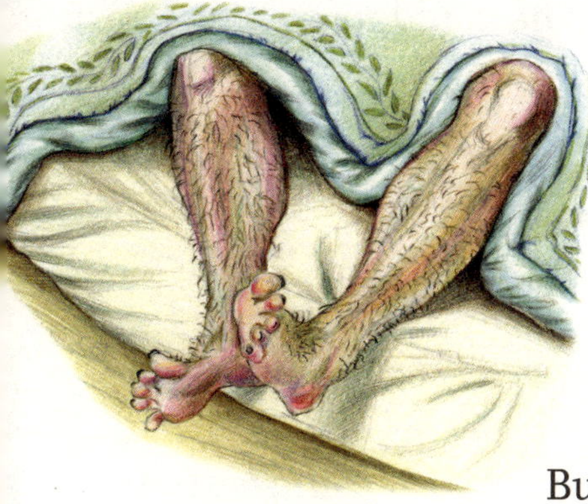

'Oh, my god, please no,' he whispered through gritted teeth.

He threw back the bedclothes and swung his legs out. But they were not his legs, not his legs at all. They were the short and strangely malformed legs of Edward Hyde. 'No!' he said again. 'This must still be a dream.'

'No, it's not a dream, my dear doctor,' a guttural voice whispered in his head. 'It's me. I'm coming again. You cannot keep me away.'

He staggered from his bed and, pulling the curtains back from the window, he saw, instead of his own reflection in the moonlight, the face of Edward Hyde glaring back at him from the glass, smiling at him. And, god help him, a part of him wanted to smile back. He knew

- grit (v.) 咬紧(牙)
- malformed (a.) 畸形的
- guttural (a.) 喉音的

now that he must do all he could to keep that part of himself under control.

♪13 From this time on, Jekyll's metabolism surged in waves of discomfort, the days frequently interrupted by terrible struggles to subdue Mr Hyde. The doctor continued to administer the restorative drug to himself, gradually increasing the quantity in order to hold the monster he had created at bay. Then, one sunny afternoon as he sat on a bench overlooking the lake in Regent's Park, he was overcome with nausea and uncontrollable shuddering. When he looked down, he saw that his trousers were in folds around his shoes and his hands were hairy and gnarled upon his knees.

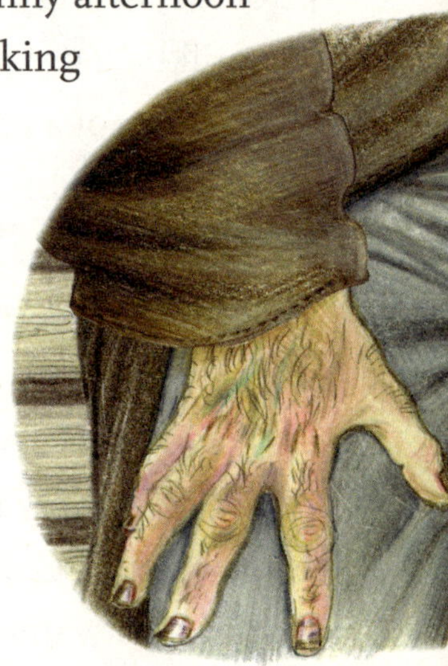

- subdue (v.) 压抑
- restorative (a.) 恢复健康的
- nausea (n.) 恶心
- shudder (v.) 发抖

In a panic, Hyde—now retaining many of the sensibilities of his alter ego—pulled his hat down further to cover his misshapen face and shrugged his coat collar higher before making for home as fast as he could. But he realised that he could not make the trip without being seen.

Perhaps his friend Dr Lanyon might help. Or possibly even Utterson, though he feared there might be little sympathy from that direction. It would have to be Lanyon: the brutal truth was that he had little or no choice.

Looking around, he spotted a hostelry where, he was sure, neither the hosts nor the customers would be bothered by his unruly appearance and his ill-fitting clothes. He stumped across the street and, within a few minutes, he had arranged for a private room and requested writing materials.

• misshapen (a.) 畸形的

• stump (v.) 笨重地行走

He promptly set about writing notes to both Lanyon and Dr Jekyll's butler, Poole—he no longer considered himself as the doctor, at least not when Hyde had overtaken him. Affecting the guise of someone suffering

• guise (n.) 伪装

from a head-cold, his collar pulled high and his scarf wrapped tightly about his lower face, he passed the notes to the innkeeper and returned to his room to wait for nightfall. As soon as darkness had filled the sky and the only lights were those cast by the meagre streetlamps now being lit, he left the inn and hailed a cab, requesting that the driver simply drive him around the darkened streets of London.

♪14 Elsewhere in the city, Dr Lanyon arrived at Jekyll's house, somewhat puzzled by the note he had received. Poole was similarly at a loss to understand what was happening, but he admitted Lanyon and led him to Dr Jekyll's laboratory.

'He asks that I take this drawer to him,' Lanyon said, his voice unsure. 'Whatever can he be wanting it for, I wonder?'

• meagre (a.) 不足的

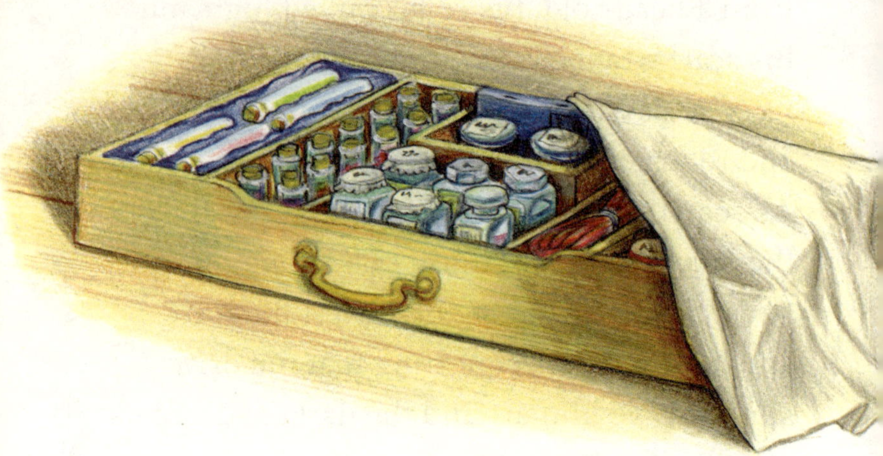

The two men paused and looked into the drawer, which was a neat arrangement of stoppered test-tubes, phials, circular tins with curious scribbles on their lids and banded confusions of rubber hose. And a book.

'I am sure I have no idea, Dr Lanyon,' Poole remarked.

Without further conversation, Lanyon took the drawer and left Jekyll's house, bound for home.

- stopper (v.) 用塞子塞住
- phial (n.) 小玻璃瓶
- tin (n.) 马口铁器皿
- scribble (n.) 草草写成的东西

♪15 Once home, Lanyon looked more closely at the contents of the drawer. The powders were neatly enough made up, but not with the nicety of the dispensing chemist, so that it was plain they were of Jekyll's private manufacture. The book contained little but a series of dates. These covered a period of many years, but the entries had ceased about a year ago, and quite abruptly.

A knock interrupted Lanyon's investigations. When he answered the door, he found a man who was clearly in something of a distressed state. The man's clothes were enormously too large for him in every measurement, the trousers hanging on his legs and rolled up to keep them from the ground, and the coat collar sprawling wide upon his shoulders.

Dr Lanyon was further struck by the haunted expression of his face, and by his apparent state of illness.

- dispensing chemist (n.) 药剂师
- sprawl (v.) 使不规则地延伸

'Edward Hyde, sir,' Hyde announced gruffly. 'I am the messenger from Dr Jekyll.'

• gruffly (adv.) 粗暴地

Lanyon was unsure what to do next, but Hyde pushed his way into the house. As soon as the door was closed behind him, he grabbed hold of Lanyon's shoulders and shook him roughly.

'Do you have it?' he asked. 'Do you have it?'

Managing to disengage himself from the unpleasant man, Lanyon frowned icily. 'You forget, sir,' he said, 'that I have not had the pleasure of your acquaintance.'

'I do beg your pardon, doctor,' Hyde said, regaining some of his composure. 'I understood that a drawer…' He stopped when he saw the object in question on Lanyon's bureau.

Hyde visibly faltered, his hands clutching his chest as he requested a glass.

'Are you not well?' Lanyon asked.

'A glass!' Hyde barked.

When Lanyon returned with the glass, Hyde mixed a fizzing potion from the ingredients before him. As he raised the glass to his mouth, Hyde turned to Lanyon and said, 'You must remember

- disengage (v.) 使脱离
- icily (adv.) 冷淡地
- bureau (n.) 书桌
- falter (v.) 摇晃

the vows you made when joining our profession, my dear Lanyon.'

Lanyon was aghast at the man's familiarity.

'What follows,' Hyde continued, oblivious to the other man's sensibilities, 'is to be our secret.' And he drained the glass before staggering forward to support himself on the bureau.

Almost immediately, the transformation began.

The thuggish Edward Hyde was slowly but surely changing into the more refined form of Henry Jekyll.

- aghast (a.) 吓呆的
- thuggish (a.) 凶残的

'What in god's name, man—?' Lanyon began.

'God has no part in tonight's events,' Hyde croaked, though his voice was becoming softer and less guttural.

When finally the process had ended, and Jekyll alone now stood by the bureau, Lanyon went across and took his friend's arm. 'Whatever was—?'

Jekyll shook his head. 'Please keep silent about what you have seen,' he said, his voice growing a little stronger.

• croak (v.) 用低哑的声音说

'You should see someone, get help.' But his friend had already disappeared into the night.

'Return the drawer, dear Lanyon,' Jekyll's disembodied voice called out of the swirling mist.

♪16 Some weeks later, Utterson received a visit from Poole, who asked that the lawyer come to the house immediately; his master, it transpired, had locked himself in his laboratory.

'He has been in there for several days now,' Poole breathlessly informed Utterson as the pair strode purposefully through town towards Jekyll's house.

'Moreover,' Poole confided, 'I am becoming increasingly concerned by what I hear from behind the locked door.'

'What sounds do you hear, dear fellow?'

'His voice, sir—it was not my master's voice.'

Sure enough, at Jekyll's house the voice that spoke in response to the butler's insistent

- disembodied (a.) 脱离现实的
- transpire (v.) 发生

knocking on the laboratory door was considerably changed—it was hoarse, guttural. 'I do not want to see anyone,' it said.

'I wonder if the devil has done away with my master,' Poole whispered.

'You say he's been in there for several days?'

Poole nodded. 'Eight days to be precise, crying and wailing like a soul demented. And all the while I have been sent hither and thither, bearing notes to all the chemists I know—and some whom I did not know.'

- wail (v.) 号啕
- dement (v.) 使发狂

'And what did these notes say?'

'They were for ingredients, sir, for some drug. Every time I brought the stuff back, there would be another note telling me to return it, because it was not pure, and another order to a different firm. He wants this drug very bad, sir, for whatever reason.'

'Do you have one of these notes?'

Frowning, the butler patted his pockets, and produced a crumpled piece of paper which he flattened out before handing to Utterson.

'And was the chemist able to produce what your master requested?' Utterson asked as he read the note.

Poole shook his head with regret. 'Alas, no. I was told that the drug which the doctor wanted was no longer available—apparently he himself had bought the last of it some time previously. So I returned home without it, at which point…' The butler stopped and glanced at the closed door. 'At which point the person in the room—for I can no

• crumple (v.) 起皱

longer assume that it is my master—grew angry.'

'Well, you should have no concerns, Poole—this is indeed the doctor's hand.'

Poole nodded enthusiastically. 'Yes, Mr Utterson,' he said at last. 'It is the doctor's hand—or, at least, a close facsimile of it—but what matter the hand? I have seen him.'

'Seen him?'

'Yes, sir. It was but for one minute, but the hair stood upon my head like quills. Sir, if that was my master, why had he a mask upon his face? If it was my master, why did he cry out like a rat, and run from me?'

'Was it Mr Hyde?'

'Yes, sir,' Poole confirmed. 'I believe it was.'

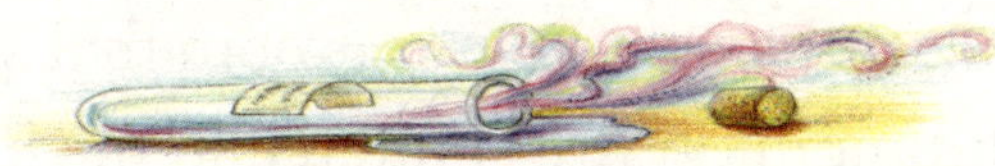

♪17 Having resolved that the only course of action was to break down the door into Jekyll's laboratory, Utterson dispatched the footman to the other entrance with instructions not to allow anyone

- facsimile (n.) 摹写
- quill (n.) 羽毛
- footman (n.) 男仆

ease of passage. Then, armed with axe and poker, they returned to the door.

'Jekyll,' Utterson called loudly. 'I demand to see you.' He paused but there was no reply. 'I give you fair warning. Our suspicions are aroused and I mean to see you. If you do not allow us access then we shall have no alternative but to break down the door.'

'Utterson,' a voice croaked from within, 'for god's sake have mercy.'

'That is not the voice of my friend,' Utterson said softly to the butler. 'It is Hyde's voice. Down with the door, Poole!'

Within minutes, Poole had brought down the heavy door with a succession of bold swings of the axe, and the pair burst into a room that seemed almost tranquil. A fire sputtered in the hearth, drawers were open, their contents visible but neat, and, by the fire, things were laid out for tea while a kettle hummed on the grate.

But in the middle of the floor lay a figure, still twitching.

- poker (v.) 拨火棒
- kettle (n.) 水壶
- grate (n.) 火炉
- twitch (v.) 抽动

Utterson bent down to turn over the figure. It was Edward Hyde, but dressed in clothes that were clearly far too big for his frame. 'I fear we are too late,' Utterson said, as he held Hyde's wrist and felt for a pulse. 'It only remains for us to find the body of your master.'

♪18 Following an extensive search, Utterson and Poole found no sign of Dr Jekyll, either alive or dead.

'Sir, there's a letter,' Poole exclaimed from the counter, 'and it's addressed to you.'

Utterson went across to the butler and opened the envelope. 'Why, it's Jekyll's will,' said Utterson. 'He has written a new one. And in place of Hyde, your master has placed my own name as beneficiary.' Utterson turned his attention to the counter and discovered a second packet, this one dated and containing two documents—one written by Jekyll himself and one by Dr Lanyon.

'Jekyll must have been here this very day,' Utterson said. 'He cannot have been killed and buried in so short a time. He must have fled, though why should he flee?'

'Perhaps the answer is in those letters,' Poole ventured.

The lawyer nodded. 'Perhaps. But I foresee

that we may yet involve your master in some dire catastrophe.'

♪19 Before the night was out, Utterson knew the full extent of his friend's folly. He had read Lanyon's account of Hyde's bizarre transformation earlier in the year. He had read Jekyll's painful disclosure of his determination to increase medical knowledge, without a single concern for his own safety or well-being. And he had read of Henry Jekyll's belief that man was not one entity but two, like the two sides of a coin, one good and one bad. 'If each,' Jekyll had written, 'could be housed in separate identities, life would be relieved of all that was unbearable.'

When he reached the end of the account, Utterson held his head in despair. Alas, his friend had discovered instead that each man must house the whole of himself—both the

- dire (a.) 可怕的
- catastrophe (n.) 大灾难

good and the bad—within one identity and one body. It is the failure to balance these opposing forces within one identity and one body that makes life truly unbearable.

TAKING THINGS FURTHER

The real read

This *Real Reads* version of *The Strange Case of Dr Jekyll and Mr Hyde* is a retelling of Robert Louis Stevenson's wonderful and rather frightening short novel. If you would like to read the full novel in all its original splendour, many complete editions are available, from bargain paperbacks to beautifully-bound hardbacks. You should be able to find a copy in your local library or in a charity shop.

Filling in the spaces

The loss of so many of Stevenson's original words is a sad but necessary part of the shortening process. Although we have omitted little, we have had to make some difficult decisions concerning the sequence of events. The points below will help you to move from this *Real Reads* version of *Dr Jekyll and Mr Hyde* to Robert Louis Stevenson's original.

- Utterson is concerned by the change in his friend's will. His attempt to understand Jekyll's motives begins the process that will eventually reveal the doctor's folly.
- When he meets Hyde for the first time, Utterson considers him deformed and even troglodytic—a troglodyte is a creature that lives below ground and away from the sunlight.
- Utterson believes that Jekyll must have committed some unspeakable crime, the details of which Hyde knows about.
- When confronted, Jekyll explains that his relationship with Hyde is 'one of those affairs that cannot be mended by talking', which suggests that Jekyll recognises very early in the story that he is in danger of losing control.
- In the original, the killing of Sir Danvers Carew is a remarkably brutal passage: 'The old gentleman took a step back, with the air of one very much surprised and a trifle hurt; and at that Mr Hyde broke out of all bounds and clubbed him to the earth. And next moment, with ape-

like fury, he was trampling his victim under foot and hailing down a storm of blows, under which the bones were audibly shattered.'

- When Inspector Newcomen goes with Utterson to Hyde's rooms they discover many signs of a double life—'A closet was filled with wine; the plate was of silver, the napery elegant; a good picture hung upon the wall', yet clothes are strewn around in heaps as though the place has been ransacked.

- Some time before the close of the story, Dr Lanyon dies following a short but aggressive illness. After his friend's death, Utterson receives a letter from Lanyon marked for his personal attention, with the additional clause 'in case of his predecease to be destroyed unread'.

- It is in Henry Jekyll's last letter, in his own words, that we learn first-hand of all the horrors he has experienced.

Back in time

Robert Louis Stevenson wrote *The Strange Case of Dr Jekyll and Mr Hyde* in 1886, at the age of thirty-six. He was already known for the exciting subject matter of his adventure novels and stories of the fantastic, such as *Treasure Island*, a thrilling adventure story of a search for buried gold. The most exciting of his books, however, and certainly the one which achieved greatest immediate acclaim, was his tale of Dr Jekyll and Mr Hyde. Within a few months it sold 40,000 copies, and as the century turned it was estimated to have sold more than 250,000.

Stevenson had long been interested in the idea of the two sides—good and evil—of human character. He lived in a society which greatly valued etiquette, reputation and proper manners. Such civilised behaviour tended to cause people to repress other sides of their characters, such as sensuality, physicality, and anger.

At the same time the British were exploring and conquering new worlds, where society often behaved differently, in a way that Victorians considered 'savage'. Whilst they might fear the 'savage', many Victorians were also fascinated, perhaps because they recognised such tendencies within themselves.

During the nineteenth century, many parts of London had become overcrowded and dirty: poverty and disease were terrible problems. People of Jekyll's class might have chosen to ignore it, but they could not have been unaware of the existence of 'less civilised' people in their midst. Stevenson wanted to explore, in the words of Dr Jekyll, 'man, not as truly one, but truly two'.

Queen Victoria's reign saw great progress in science, technology and medicine. By 1886 anaesthetics and antiseptic were in common use, and people were increasingly interested in the potential of science, which led to considerable experimentation. This gave Stevenson the medical background to his story.

Once Stevenson had found a way to write about the two sides of human nature, he attacked the project with such ferocity that the entire book was probably completed in as little as three days.

Food for thought

Here are some things to think about if you are reading *The Strange Case of Dr Jekyll and Mr Hyde* or ideas for discussion if you are reading it with friends.

In retelling the story we have tried to recreate, as accurately as possible, Robert Louis Stevenson's original plot and characters. We have also tried to imitate aspects of his style. Remember, however, that this is not the original work; thinking about the points below, therefore, can only help you begin to understand the author's craft. To move forward from here, turn to the full-length version and lose yourself in his exciting tale.

Starting points

- Give examples from the text of the way the author uses the city itself as a character to create moods.
- Would you say that Utterson is a helpful

and well-meaning character, or do you think he comes across as nosy and interfering?

- Why do you think there are no women characters in Stevenson's book? What do you think about the fact that none of the main characters seems to be in an important relationship?

- What do you think are the aspects of Hyde that give most concern to those who encounter him.

Themes

What do you think Robert Louis Stevenson is saying about the following themes?

- the two sides of human nature
- civilised society and human beings
- scientific experiments
- friendship and honesty

Style

Can you find paragraphs containing examples of the following?

- the use of exclamation marks
- descriptions of scenery
- the use of short sentences to create suspense
- sentences that use old-fashioned language

Look closely at how these paragraphs are written. What do you notice? Can you write a paragraph in the same style?

POST-READING

读有所得

《化身博士》的故事世界闻名，书中的杰科尔博士是个典型的悲剧人物。他是一个拥有丰厚遗产、具有强健身体而且头脑聪明的科学家。他在科学领域里获得了巨大的成就。所有的人都把杰科尔博士看成一本正经、勤奋工作、令人尊敬的博士。但是他的内心却并非是外表所表现出来的样子。 他的内心被他的名誉、成就、人品严重地束缚住，真实想法一直被压抑着， 直到有一天他的研究成功了。通过药物， 他变成了另外一个人，他就像一只笼中鸟，或者更确切地说， 是一头出笼的野兽。他杀了人，却无比畅快。他的欲望得到了无限的释放， 一直压抑在心中的邪恶被激发了出来。杰科尔博士一直依靠药物变化身份， 可慢慢地善与恶的冲突却在他的身上体现得越加明显，直到他最终被恶全部占领。药物也不能再起作用，杰科尔博士忏悔了，最终离开了人世。

这本书具有强烈的科幻和恐怖色彩，情节紧凑连贯， 引人入胜。 在通读全文之后，读者们就会发现书中出现了很多我们本来认识的单词，但是在这本书中却赋予了它们新的意思，现在我们就进入《化身博士》这本书，一起来学习新知识吧。

一、旧词新义或一词多义

1. “indeed？” Utterson remarked… (p.1)

remark一般情况下，我们见到这个词，意思为“评论”，词性为名词。但是在这句中，很明显它的意思为“说”。实际上在英文表达中，有很多词都有“说”的意思。例如：he said；he adds；he puts；he declared等。这需要读者们平时在阅读时对词汇进行总结和积累。

2. …I collared him and then called a doctor to the scene to attend the child.（p.2）

collar 意思是“领子”，词性为名词。这句话中明显它是作为动词使用的，意思需要引申成“抓住某人的衣领”。而第二个词attend，我们通常看到这个词就知道它的意思是“参加”，几乎相当于“take part in”或“participate in”的意思。但是将这个意思放在这句话中就说不通了，原来attend 还有另外一个意思是“照顾某人”。

3. He leafed through them until he found an envelope

bearing the words…(p.4)

从开始接触英语，大家都知道leaf是树叶的意思，但是这里显然为动词，意思为“翻阅”。 而第二个词bear， 我们知道它的名词意思为“熊”， 而动词意思为“忍受”， 但是在这句话中，通过上下文我们可以轻易地得知， bear 在这里的意思是“写道”。在之后的阅读中我们也会发现， 这里在表达“通知上写着……”

这句的英文表达是：“the note reads…”， 而不是使用中文思维中， 我们认为的“write”一词。

4. A man appeared out of the gloom into the small pool of gaslight, reached into his pocket, and produced a key.（p.6）

我们都知道reach 是“到达”的意思， 但是，其实在表达把手伸进兜里的时候， 通常都是用“reach”这个词的。 而produce 原本是“生产”的意思， 这里的意思是手在兜里摸出了一把钥匙。

5. I thought you might admit me. （p.7）

admit 一词原意是“允许”， 在此处意思为“允许某人进入家中”。

6. …I shall need his address in order to fulfill the terms

of Dr. Jekyll’s will?（p.8）

address 一词在句中意思为“地址”，这个意思众所周知，但是还有些时候，我们会见到这个词作动词，意思为“处理”，相当于“handle 或者deal with”。在这里提及一下，希望大家下次再见到这个词的时候，能够马上想到它的动词含义。而will，多数情况下，我们所熟知的是它可以作为一般将来时的标志词，但是在这篇作品中的will大都是指“遗嘱”。

7. What on earth could possibly link Jekyll with such an unpleasant man…（p.9）

earth 是“地球”的意思，但是on earth 连在一起却和地球没有任何关系。这个词组的意思是“到底”。

8. He decided that there was only one course left open to him. (p.9)

course一词我们最熟知的意思是“课程”，其实它还有很多意思，比如：in the course of 表示“在……的过程中”，而在这句话中，course 的意思为“道路”。

9. One house still wore a great air of wealth and comfort…(p.9)

wore 是动词wear 的过去式形式，意思是“穿戴着……”， air一词， 相信没有读者不认识， 但是在句中， 两个词的意思都发生了一些变化。 整句的意思理解为： 整栋房子弥漫着富贵和舒适的气息。

10. Your master seems to have placed a great deal of trust in this fellow···(p.10)

place 作为名词， 意思为“地点”， 作为动词可引申为“放置”。 在这句中的意思是： 你的主人似乎对这个人相当地信任。 也可以理解成“给予”。

11.‘with regard to what, my dear friend?’ (p.11)

regard原意为“问候”，但是词组的意思却大相径庭。with regard to 意思是“关于”。再补充两个词组也有“关于”的含义： as for和with respect to。

12. ···you will look after him and his rights.（p.11）

right 一词用得最多的两个意思应该是on the right 在右边， 还有you are right你是对的。 但是在这句中，rights 意思为权力和权益。 此句的意思是：“你将要照顾他， 并且保障他的权益。”

13. ···Henry Jekyll was flooded with regret. (p.14)

flood 一词原意为“洪水”，在这里形象地表明后悔的情绪像洪水般涌入心里。

14. …Of course, by all means—take the blessed thing away. (p.21)

He meant to murder you. (p.21)

第一句中的means 意思是“方法”。means 中的s并不是这个词的复数形式。by all means 这一词组的意思是“当然，务必”。还有一个词组是by no means，其意思是“绝不”。

第二句中的mean，词性是动词，意思是“想要，打算”。

精彩片段解析

1. In the lamplight, Utterson noticed how Hyde's brows met in thick black hair and his face was pale, the eyes glinting like those of a fish–barely human, in fact. (p.7)

译文：在灯光的照射下，阿特森注意到，海德粗黑的两道眉毛连成了一条线，他的脸色苍白如雪，眼睛像鱼眼一样闪烁；简直可以说，一点儿也不像一个人。

解析：这句中作者用简短的语言描绘出了海德的外貌特征。例如：他的眉毛连成一条线，他的脸色苍白，眼睛像鱼眼，都是非常形象的描写。而最后一句对于他外貌的总结更是点睛之笔。根本不像个人类，更是说明了通过药物而变成的邪恶怪物是多么的丑陋。在人物的外貌描写中，读者们应该学会的是外貌特征不需要描写得面面俱到，而是抓住面目中的最主要特征进行描写，才会起到令人印象深刻的效果。

2. Almost immediately he slumped against the heavy wooden counter, his face a mask of pain. Eyes tightly shut and mouth clenched, he clutched his stomach and folded over, stifling a deep moan. Even as he bent forward, his body was already thickening, changing—sinew, muscle, artery, all of them expanding or contracting. Churning noises rumbled from his stomach, cartilage and bone twanged and cracked as his neck grew shorter and his neatly-styled hair exploded into a dense thatch. (p.13)

译文: 一喝完，他立刻倒靠在厚重的木头长桌上，脸上呈现出痛苦的表情。双眼紧闭，咬牙切齿，他紧握住他的胃部，蜷缩着身体，发出了低沉的呻吟声。在他整个人往前倾的时候，他的身体逐渐变得更加厚实——肌腱、肌肉、动脉等所有的器官都在扩张或收缩，他的腹部发出绞动的声音。他的软骨和骨头因碰撞嘎嘎作响，同时他的脖子变得越来越短，他梳理整齐的头发，也倏地变成一头稻草似的乱发。

解析：这一段的描写非常精彩，主要描写的是杰科尔博士变身成为海德的全过程。整段的用词并不算多，但是却给人触目惊心、身临其境之感。这段描写的精彩之处主要是通过动词和象声词的运用而营造出来的。例如：slump 重摔在桌上；clench 咬紧嘴唇；clutch 紧紧抓住；rumble隆隆作响；twang 嘎嘎作响；crack 破裂的噼啪声。读者们可以通过读书，加强对动词的学习和使用。

（解析主讲人：胡迪）

CHINESE TRANSLATION

中文翻译

人物介绍

亨利·杰科尔博士

这位备受尊崇的博士，能否抗拒海德先生诡异的力量呢？

爱德华·海德

这个男子到底是什么人？他究竟对杰科尔博士有什么神秘的控制力呢？

阿特森先生

阿特森先生是杰科尔博士的朋友，同时也是他的律师。他能解开这个谜团吗？他能拯救他的朋友吗？

理察・恩菲尔德

理察・恩菲尔德掌握着哪些资讯呢？他是要拯救杰科尔博士，还是要宣告杰科尔博士有罪？

普尔

普尔是杰科尔博士忠心耿耿的管家。他能否拯救主人免予自我戕害呢？

哈斯蒂・蓝扬博士

蓝扬博士亲眼目睹了一桩光怪陆离的惊人事件。他会有什么样的反应？

纽卡曼警官

纽卡曼警官是优秀的苏格兰场警察。他能不能发现爱德华・海德的真实身份，侦破这桩凶残的谋杀案？

p.1 “你知道吗？”恩菲尔德对他的律师朋友阿特森说。他们两人正漫步在伦敦的落后地区，他接着说：“在我的脑海中，那边那栋房子与一桩诡异的故事密不可分。”

“真的吗？”阿特森边说边仔细注视着他朋友所指的那栋不祥的建筑。“告诉我是怎么回事。”

“有一天我很晚回家，那是某个冬夜的凌晨，大约三点，我回家的路得经过这个地区。就在这里，也就是我们现在站立的这个地方，我看到了最诡异的事情。有个人泰然自若地践踏一个小女孩，任由她在地上尖叫。”

“为了什么原因？”

恩菲尔德摇摇头，“不为什么，她只是不小心撞到了他。”

“所以是那个女孩子的错了？”

p.2 “或许吧。但这个男人，这个令人发指的家伙，就想这样走掉。我抓住他的领口，然后打电话给一位医生，请他到现场来照料这个孩子。”

“那个家伙喝醉了吗？”

“据我所知没有。人群逐渐围拢聚集，喊着要给他放点儿血，但我和医生阻止了他们。”

“那这栋房子，”阿特森说，“跟这件事有什么关系？”

“女孩的父母威胁要起诉——这个官司他们一定可以打赢的——于是我们尽力说服他支付一百英镑的赔偿金，来弥补他的过错。刚开始这家伙不太愿意，但我猜
p.3 他最后畏惧群众的压力，于是他引领我们到这栋房子，他消失在里面，出来后带着十英镑的硬币，还有一张支票，把金额补足。

“哼！”阿特森不屑地说：“我敢打赌那张支票是……”

“不，”恩菲尔德打断他，“我自己也有疑虑，但是我们全都聚集在我家里，一直待到银行开门。我们去了银行，银行工作人员确认那张支票是真的，那家人也拿到了他们的九十英镑。”

“这件事就这样结束了？”

恩菲尔德耸耸肩，点点头。两人又继续往前走。

“那家伙叫什么名字？”

“海德，”恩菲尔德用很小的声音回答，“爱德华·海德。但是支票上的名字并不是这个。”

阿特森的脚步再度停下。“你是说，爱德华·海德？”

恩菲尔德点点头，“有什么不对吗，亲爱的阿特森？”

p.4 “没什么，亲爱的老友。我刚刚一度以为我认识这家伙，或者应该说我知道他。”

他们一路走，经过一道防波堤，有一个小男孩坐在上面，手中的鱼线抛入了黑暗的河水里。恩菲尔德说：“你没问我支票上的名字。”

阿特森点点头，露齿微笑，几秒钟之后他才说：“因为我相信我已经知道了。”他没说出口的是，他知道那栋房子的主人是谁，那栋房子的后门正是恩菲尔德所指向的那个门。

阿特森一回到家，便迫不及待地从保险柜里拿出一些文件。他一张张翻着，找到了一个信封，上面写着：“亨利·杰科尔之遗嘱”。他将信封打开，在摇曳闪烁的烛光下阅读，他找到了他要找的句子：一旦杰科尔博士死亡，其所有财产将留给博士的“好友兼恩人”爱德华·海德。不止如此，接着文件还写着：假如博士消失超过三个月的时间，海德将完全继承亨利·杰科尔的所有财物。除了支付博士家用的几笔小开销以外，其他所有财务义务，他将不需负担。

“我不知道到底发生什么事了，也不知道这位叫海德的家伙到底抓住你什么把柄了，亨利·杰科尔，”阿特森在房里喃喃自语，“但是我发誓我会把它当作自己的事，尽全力去找出真相。”

接下来的几天，阿特森的确把这件事当作自己的事，一有时间就到他朋友恩菲尔德所指出的那栋建筑附p.6近探查。他心想，假如他叫作海德先生（编者按：意指隐藏），那我就是寻觅先生。

有一天晚上，十点多的时候，他的耐心等候终于有了回报。他听到街道上回荡着脚步声，阿特森躲到一家商店的门口等着。有一个男子从阴暗处现身，走入一小团煤气灯光下。他把手探入口袋，摸出一把钥匙。他的身形矮小，几乎可以说是发育不良；他的穿着平实，他的脸被遮蔽在帽檐之下。尽管他鬼鬼祟祟地四下张望，

但还是没有发现阿特森，直到他穿过街道，几乎到了家门口时才看到阿特森。

“我想你是海德先生吧？”阿特森从阴暗处走出来，轻声地说。

p.7 这男子猛然倒抽一口气并往后退，但还是设法不让自己的脸被看到。“你有什么事？”他问道，口气不善。

阿特森朝门口点了点头说：“我是杰科尔博士的朋友，我想我们可以到屋里谈一谈。”

“你是谁？”

“我是阿特森，住在刚特街。”阿特森说，“你应该听过我的名字。”海德摇了摇头，阿特森继续说：“我以为你会让我进去。”

“杰科尔博士不在家，他出门去了。你怎么会认识我？”

阿特森没有回答那个问题，反而问了另一个问题：“你能否帮我个忙？”

“什么忙？”海德怀着戒心询问道。

“能不能让我看看你的脸？”这位律师问。

爱德华·海德犹豫了一下，然后，仿佛突然改变心意似的，他以一种反抗的态度直直盯着阿特森。在灯光p.8 的照射下，阿特森注意到，海德粗黑的两道眉毛连成一条线，他的脸色苍白如雪，眼睛像鱼眼一样闪烁；简直可以说，一点儿都不像是个人。

“这样我应该可以认得出你了，”阿特森说，“应该有点儿帮助。”

“是的，”海德回答，“或许我们以前见过，我想你应该也有我的地址。”他给了律师一个在苏活区的街道号码。“老天啊，”阿特森心想，“他以为我需要他的地址以便去履行杰科尔博士的遗嘱吗？”

“现在你可以告诉我，你怎么认识我的了吧？”海德说。

“首先，我们有共同认识的朋友，”阿特森说，“就是杰科尔博士。”

海德的眼睛瞪得很大。“杰科尔跟你说了我什么事？”他带着怒气大吼。海德不等对方回答，就把门打开，头也不回地进入屋里，消失无踪了。

p.9 阿特森不禁纳闷，杰科尔怎么会跟这样一个脾气暴躁的人有所关联？不管是为了什么，至少有一件事是确定的，他们两个人的关系，对于博士来说只有坏处，不会有好处。现在阿特森只剩下一条路可以走，他务必去找亨利·杰科尔谈一谈了。

在这栋邪恶建筑的转角处，也就是海德消失的地方，有一排古老气派的房子，已经有点儿破旧了。其中一栋房子仍带有富裕和舒适的氛围，尽管现在除了天窗以外，整栋屋子完全陷入黑暗中。阿特森先生驻足在大门前，然后敲了门。

不一会儿，杰科尔的老管家前来开门，他略微驼背但听力仍然很好，见
p.10 到阿特森他立刻笑逐颜开。

“噢，是阿特森先生。”管家愉悦地说，“不巧主人出门了。”

阿特森先生点点头，懊恼地说：“没关系，普尔，我下次再来看他。”然后他又说，“今天稍早，我好像看到海德先生从以前的解剖室进来，当时博士不在，是不是这样？”

“一点儿也没错，先生。那位先生有钥匙。”

“你的主人似乎对这个人相当信任。”阿特森一边说着，一边转身向台阶走去。

“是的，先生，”普尔附和道，“主人吩咐我们所有人要听从他的命令，尽管如此，但他却从没在此用过餐，我们甚至很少在屋子里看到他。他大多数时候都从实验室进出。”

在穿越漫漫浓雾走回家的途中，阿特森先生心头纷乱。直到抵达熟悉的家门口并进入屋内，他才感到开心起来。

p.11 “亨利，我一直想找你谈谈。”阿特森说。在杰科尔博士所举办的一场很棒的晚宴上，他一直留到最后，喝完最后一杯酒。

“谈哪方面的事呢，我亲爱的朋友？”

“有关你的遗嘱。”阿特森回答。

杰科尔用鼻子哼了一声，“我的遗嘱？”

“是的，有关海德。我听到一些关于他的事。”

杰科尔站了起来，“说来听听。”

“但我听到的是……”

杰科尔挥挥手，“不，你不明白我的立场，我的处境有点儿……有点儿不知如何是好。简单地说，我在这件事上的立场很奇怪。我知道你见过他了。”杰科尔继续说，“他告诉我了，而我担心他对你不礼貌。不过，我还是要请你承诺，万一哪天我不在世上了，你会照顾他，保障他的权益。”

阿特森知道再说什么都没用了，因为他的朋友主意已定。“我无法假装自己喜欢他这个人。”他轻声地说。

p.12 “我不要求你这么做，我只要求一切合法。”

“很好，”阿特森最后说，“我答应你。”

杰科尔目送着他的朋友消失在街道上，之后，他先去确认大门是否已经锁上，然后交代普尔，他不希望被人打扰，随即进入了他的实验室。

在他的实验室里，有一个摆满了冒着泡泡的量管和

烧瓶的架子，博士从其中拿出了一小排玻璃瓶，他把玻璃瓶里的液体，全倒进一个玻璃杯里，仔细地搅拌。等
p.13 到他觉得搅拌均匀了，便把玻璃杯拿到嘴边，他停顿了一瞬间，然后就仰头把液体倒入嘴里，一饮而尽。

一喝完，他立刻倒靠在厚重的木头长桌上，脸上呈现出痛苦的表情，双眼紧闭，咬牙切齿。他紧紧抓住他的胃，并环抱着，发出了低沉的呻吟声。在他整个人往前倾的时候，他的身体逐渐变得更厚实——肌腱、肌肉、动脉等，所有器官都在扩张或收缩，他的腹部发出扭搅的声音。他的软骨和骨头因碰撞嘎嘎作响，同时他的脖子变得越来越短，他梳理整齐的头发，也倏地变
p.14 成一头稻草似的乱发。就在发生变化的这短短几秒钟之内，亨利·杰科尔充满悔恨；不过，当改变完成之时，就没有任何后悔的余念了。就像是痛苦已被抚平了一般，他长久保有的日常身份，以及此身份所带来的诸多限制，感觉通通离开他了，取而代之的，是挣脱社会规范所钳制的一种全然的灵活。他感觉到嘴角逐渐绽开了一抹微笑。

亨利·杰科尔，本是该教区受人尊敬的医生和绅士，此刻变成了爱德华·海德。全世界以及世上所有不受约束的欢乐，已经全都属于他了。

p.15 他的身形已剧烈改变了，他换上了适合目前身材的衣服，蹑手蹑脚地，在确定自己没有吵醒普尔后，他潜进了无边的黑夜之中。

阿特森已经对他的朋友拍胸脯保证过了，所以没理由继续追逐爱德华·海德。接下来的几个月，他把精力全部放在自己的工作上。

阿特森不时会和杰科尔碰面，但也许不如以往那么热络。杰科尔解释他太忙于工作以及费时的研究了，至于研究的内容，他则总是守口如瓶。

然而，杰科尔没有告诉阿特森的就是，他可以一直服用那种神奇的药水，而不会产生任何严重的副作用；
p.16 也因此，他过着双重的生活。然而，一开始勇敢的科学实验，很快就变成了不可自拔的疯狂沉溺。慢慢地，杰科尔的新陈代谢系统越来越适应药效，而且他也越来越喜欢海德先生的性情，因此，每当杰科尔博士要变回他这个比较有责任感的自己时，他就必须加重剂量。但是，他却未能预见这将是改变一切的可怕事件。

在阿特森对杰科尔博士谈起他朋友的事之后，过了一年左右，伦敦因为一桩骇人听闻的凶杀案而闹得沸沸扬扬。大家对细节所知甚少，但已足以让人闻风丧胆。有一位女佣，住在离河边不远的房子里，某晚大约十一点时，她已上楼准备睡觉了。她不经意地从窗户望了出去，看到一位打扮邋遢的壮汉，遇到一位正在散步、衣着体面的绅士。

p.17 她立刻认出这位邋遢的男子正是爱德华·海德，因为他偶尔会来拜访她的主人。她看到那位相对之下衣着体面的绅士举起帽子打招呼。虽然她听不到两人在说什么，但她觉得应该只是礼貌性的对话。因此她看到海德后来竟突然发飙时，感到非常惊讶。海德毫不留情地把他的手杖当作军刀挥舞，攻击那位绅士。

海德把这位可怜的家伙击倒在地，还在他的胸膛跳

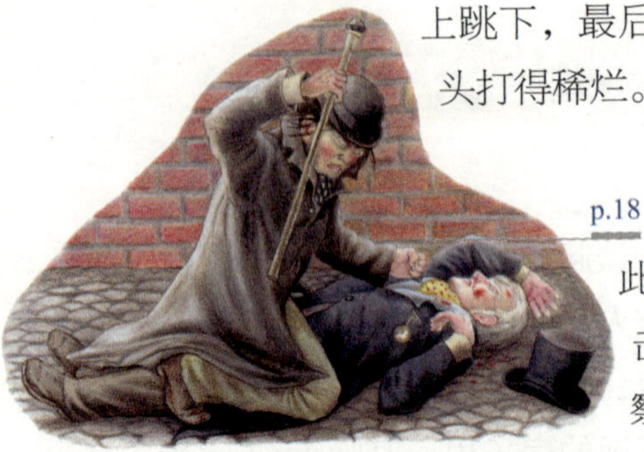

上跳下，最后，跨坐在他身上，将他的头打得稀烂。

p.18 女佣目睹了整个过程，因此能够详细地提供给警方攻击者的特征及姓名。一位警察在犯罪现场找到了一截沾满血迹的手杖。在那位身份不明的受害者身上的口袋里，找到了一封盖了邮戳的信封，上面写着阿特森的名字。于是警方去找阿特森，而这位律师要求去认尸。

“这正是我所担忧的，”阿特森说，他的话语带着沉重懊恼的情绪，“他是我很好的朋友丹佛斯·卡鲁爵士。”他对停尸间的工作人员点了点头，工作人员便把尸体盖上。“若你跟我一起上车，”他对资深警员说，“我可以带你去凶手的家。”于是他带路到苏活区的一个特定的地址去。

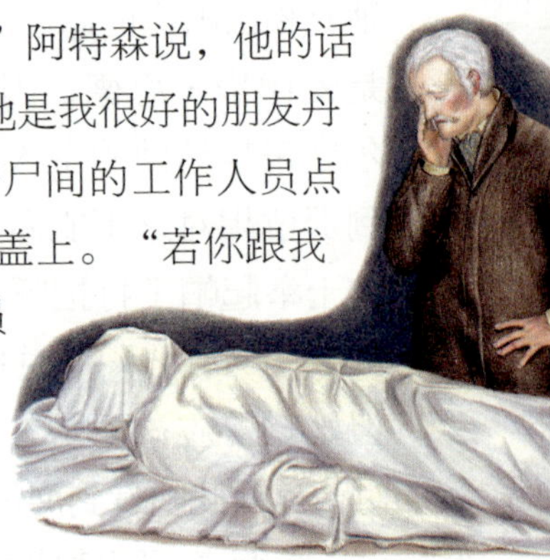

p.19 一位头发凌乱，衣着不整的老妇人前来应门。“喔，”她用粗哑低沉的声音咕哝着说，“他不在。”她似乎不太想让这些人进到屋内，但是，当苏格兰场的纽卡曼警官走向前时，她就让步了。事实上，她知道自己的主人可能犯了法，而她似乎还挺高兴的。

海德的房间一团乱，衣服堆成一座山，口袋也都外翻出来，简直就像有小
p.20 偷光顾过一样。但是，在这片混乱当中，他们找到了另一截手杖，而且，在壁炉里还有一本尚未完全烧尽的支票簿。他们去海德的银行查询，发现他的户头里有好几千英镑。

那天下午，阿特森到亨利·杰科尔的家去拜访，表明希望博士不要窝藏凶手。

“我当然不会这么做，”杰科尔告诉他的朋友。然后，他略带尴尬地补充，“而且我可以向你保证，那个人永远不会再出现了。”

为了支持这个说法，杰科尔拿出了一封他当天收到的信。这封信是海德写的，字迹就像是小孩子一样，潦草到几乎难以辨认。信件的内容只有短短几行，海德感谢杰科尔对他的支持，并解释他有办法可以逃离这座城市。他永远不会再跟杰科尔联络了。

p.21 听到了这些，阿特森觉得放心了，但是，他还是提出想看看那封信的信封。杰科尔一听就变得很有防御心，“要做什么？我已经把它烧掉了，”他大叫，“但是这信封上，绝对没有线索可以找到这家伙的下落。”

“信封一定有邮戳不是吗？”博士用力地摇摇头，“这封信是有人亲自送达的。”

“这封信能不能让我带走？”

“他的信？当然可以，没问题，把这该死的东西带走吧。”

“还有一件事：是不是海德命令你立下有关失踪的遗嘱？”阿特森问。博士似乎感到一阵晕眩，他紧紧地闭上嘴，并且点头。

“我就知道。”阿特森说，“他本来想杀你，还好你躲得好。”

p.22

“我的收获不止这样，”博士严肃地回应，“我学到一个教训，阿特森。我学到一个大教训啊！”他以手掩住面好一会儿。

当阿特森穿戴好外套和帽子的时候，杰科尔的心情已经好多了。

“对了，有件较开心的事。这个月内，不知您能否赏脸找一天与我共进晚餐？”

阿特森欣然答应了，而博士承诺会寄一封正式的邀请函，提醒他的朋友聚餐的安排及日期。

在走出大门之前，阿特森问普尔，那位帮海德送信来的人，长什么样子。

“什么送信的人？阿特森先生，今天没有人送信来啊。”

“你确定吗，普尔？”

"非常确定，先生。"

p.23 回到了办公室，阿特森将下午的经历讲述给他的事务主任盖斯特先生听，盖斯特先生认为海德一定是疯子。阿特森拿出海德的信给盖斯特看。

"不，或许他不是疯子，但他的笔迹确实相当怪异。"

就在这个时候，阿特森的男仆送进来一封短笺，那是杰科尔博士的聚餐邀请函。盖斯特刚好瞥见，便请求阿特森让他看一下。男仆将短笺递过来，盖斯特把它放在桌上，就正好摆在海德的信件旁。他突然一脸不可置信的表情，转头看着阿特森。盖斯特将两封信移到阿特森眼前起，让阿特森看。"阿特森先生，尽管这两封信的字迹有一些显著的差异，但在我看来，我觉得两者之间有很明确的相似性。"

"相似性？"阿特森欠身向前，他先看了看他的朋友亨利·杰科尔那个熟悉的工整笔迹，然后再看爱德

p.24 华·海德孩子般参差不齐的潦草字迹，甚至可以说像是醉汉所写出来的字。“我实在看不出这两种字迹有何相似之处。”

盖斯特把两封信叠在一起，指出某些元素，像是以“ing”结尾的字最后的花体写法、字母“i”上那个点的位置、“A”和“H”这两个大写字母上面的那一笔横杠的笔法，同样略带浮夸。

“我的天啊！”阿特森唯一能说的就是这句。这表示他的朋友替凶手伪造了信笺吗？他把那封据称是爱德华·海德所写的信，妥善地放置在保险柜里，然后进入房里休息了。

p.25 不久，警方就提出悬赏，若有人提供海德下落就可得到奖金，但是没人出来领赏。

日子一天一天、一周一周，接着一个月又一个月地

过去了。在这段时间内，杰科尔博士又重拾以往的热情，也恢复了健康，并重新和过去已渐行渐远的朋友维系好关系。

然而，在这看似美好的表面之下，他的心中却有一股欲望不时地搅动着：他想再次变成海德，不想受到文明社会的钳制。每当他看着镜中的自己时，仿佛看到面容狰狞的爱德华·海德，正在睥睨着他，怂恿他再调配一剂新的邪恶血清药剂。

最后，博士终于屈服了——一位与稳重端庄的杰科尔博士截然不同的男子，偷偷溜出房门，走向雾气弥漫的伦敦街头，踏入鹅卵石子铺成的巷道内。

p.26 稍晚，就在这个宿命安排的夜晚，爱德华·海德看到一名刚从一间酒吧出来的男子，正走在回家的路上。他在墙后等待着那名男子，然后突然现身在他面前。

“晚安。”海德说。

正当这名男子感觉不悦之时，海德高举手杖猛击这家伙的头，在他已

p.27 经倒卧在血泊中时，海德又继续重击了三次。海德不假思索，立刻取走了那男子的钱包，最后又以双手握住手杖，再度对着那已无生命迹象的脸庞挥击，然后仓皇奔入夜色中。

海德又再次安全回到杰科尔的实验室里，他调配了一些药水饮下，然后随着玻璃杯碎了一地，海德也倒卧在地上。等他苏醒过来，他又恢复医生的身份了。“喔，上帝啊，”他啜泣着，双手紧握，仿佛祷告一般，“帮助我停止发生在我身上的这一切吧。”

p.28 几天之后，杰科尔已经能够克制住再度调配药水的冲动了。尽管很不容易，但他慢慢地回归到之前的正常生活，他待在家里，每天的生活就是动手术、独自用餐以及浸淫在他最爱的书海中。

然后，有一天晚上，他做了一个奇怪的梦。在梦中，他的皮肤就像被蛆爬满了一样，也就是他手术后用来清理开刀伤口用的蛆。他可以感觉到蛆在他的手臂、大腿、脖子和脸上蠕动着，但不知为何，他又觉得这些蛆其实好像就存在于自己的体内。他猛然坐起身子，瞪大双眼，神色紧张，扫视着被月光笼罩的房间。到底是什么事让他突然惊醒？

当念头一成形，一阵剧烈的腹痛使他弯身不起，他靠着坚定的意志力克制自己大声呼喊，因为他不希望普尔闻声冲进他的房间来。

P.29

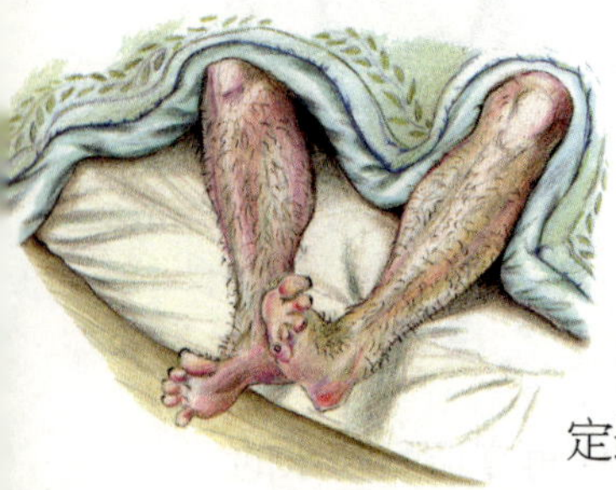

“喔，我的天，请不要这样！”他咬着牙，低声叹道。他再将床单盖在身上，只把腿露出来。但这并不是他的腿，一点都不像他的腿。这双短短的、奇形怪状的腿，根本就是爱德华·海德的腿。“不！”他又说了一次，“我一定还在做梦。”

“不，你不是在做梦，我亲爱的博士。”突然有一个低沉的喉音从他的脑海中冒出，“是我，我又回来了，你摆脱不了我的。”

他从床上蹒跚畏缩地爬起，把窗户上的窗帘拉开。

在月光下，他看到的不是他自己的倒影，而是爱德华·海德的脸从玻璃窗上回看着他，还对着他微笑。而且，上帝保佑，有一部分的他，竟也想要报以微笑。他现在
p.30 明白，他必须尽一切努力，才能避免那部分的自己失去控制。

从这个时候开始，杰科尔新陈代谢紊乱，在每天的生活里，他经常得放下手边的工作，与想要成为海德先生的冲动拼命缠斗。博士持续为自己配制复原药剂，并逐渐增加药量，以便将自己所创造出的怪物压制住。后来，在一个艳阳高照的午后，当他坐在海滩上，眺望着摄政公园里的湖面时，他有一股恶心想吐的感觉，并不由自主地颤抖起来了。他往下看，看到自己的长裤裤管堆叠覆盖在鞋子上，他毛茸茸又长满瘤节的手垂放在膝盖上。

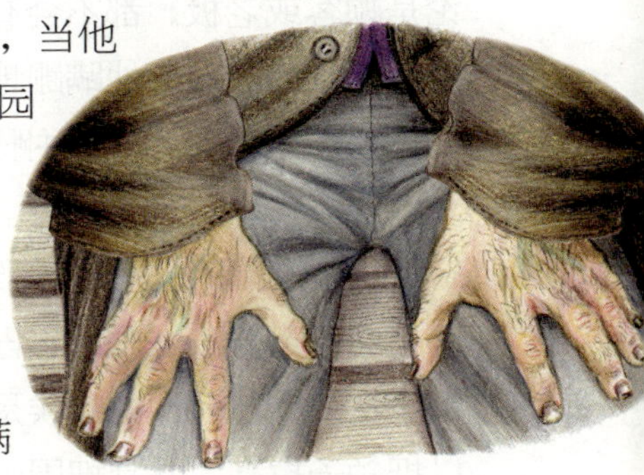

p.31 此刻，博士又再度化身为海德，但还保有另一个自

我的理性特质。他慌慌张张地压低帽檐，以遮掩他畸形的脸，并把他的外衣领子拉高，然后尽可能地快步冲回家。但他知道，这一路上不可能不被人看见。

或许他的朋友蓝扬博士可以帮忙；或者也可以找阿特森先生帮忙，不过恐怕从他那里得不到太多的同情。所以还是应该找蓝扬，老实说，杰科尔博士实在没多少选择，甚至可以说是别无选择。

环顾四周，他发现了一间旅店，他很确定在那里不论是顾客或老板，都不会有人在意他与众不同的外表以及不合身的衣服。他蹒跚地穿过街道，并在几分钟内，安排了一间单人房间，并跟老板要了书写文具。

p.32 他立刻着手写了两封短笺，分别给蓝扬和杰科尔博士的管家普尔——他不再认为自己是杰科尔博士了，
p.33 至少在海德主控他的时候是如此。他假装患了感冒，所以把领子拉高，并且把围巾紧紧地缠绕着脸的下半部，他将信笺递给旅店老板，然后回到他的房间等待黑夜降临。当夜幕遮蔽天空，此时唯一的亮光，只有街上刚

被点亮的几盏昏暗的街灯，他立即离开旅店，召了一辆马车，吩咐车夫只要载他绕行暗夜笼罩的伦敦街道就可以了。

在城市的另一方，蓝扬博士抵达了杰科尔的宅邸，对于自己所收到的信笺有点儿摸不着头绪。普尔也同样猜不透这到底是怎么一回事，但还是先让蓝扬进屋，并领他到杰科尔博士的实验室里。

“他要我带这个抽屉去给他。”蓝扬说着，声音充满了不确定，“我搞不懂他要这个做什么？”

p.34 这两个男人停顿下来查看抽屉里的东西，里面是排列得整整齐齐密封好的试管、玻璃管、盖子上有潦草字迹的圆形铁盒、一捆捆杂乱的橡皮管子，以及一本记事簿。

“我真的一点儿头绪都没有，蓝扬博士。”普尔如此说道。

蓝扬没多说什么，直接拿走抽屉，就离开杰科尔的宅邸，回自己的家了。

p.35

一回到家，蓝扬立刻更仔细地察看抽屉里的东西。那些药粉看来是研制出来的，但又不像是经由专业药剂师精制而成，所以一定是杰科尔自己调制出来的成品。那个本子记载的内容不多，只有一堆日期，而且记录了好几年的时间，但这些记录在一年前就突然地中断了。

就在蓝扬专注地研究时，一声敲门声打断了他。他开了门，看到一名相当潦倒的男子站在门口。他的衣服不管怎么看都太大，长裤宽松地垂挂在他的腿上，裤管还卷起以免拖到地上，而大衣的衣领也大大地张开，耷拉在他的肩膀上。

接着，他脸上焦虑不安的表情，以及明显的病容，立刻将蓝扬博士震慑住了。

p.36 “我是爱德华·海德，”海德粗鲁地说明来意，“我是杰科尔博士差来的。”

p.37 蓝扬还未确定接下来该怎么做，海德已经径自走向屋内。等到门一关上，海德立刻紧紧抓住蓝扬的肩膀，粗暴地摇晃。

“你拿到了没有？”他问，“有没有拿到？”

蓝扬努力挣脱这个讨厌的家伙，态度冷淡，带着不悦的语气说：“你忘了吗，先生，我还没那个荣幸认识你呢。”

“请原谅我，博士，”海德说着，同时努力恢复镇静，“我知道有一个抽屉……”当他看见书桌上放着他要的东西时，他便沉默下来。

海德整个人颤抖起来，双手交叠在胸前，支支吾吾地请求要一个玻璃杯。

“你不舒服吗？”蓝扬问道。

“一个玻璃杯！”海德大吼。

当蓝扬拿着玻璃杯回来时，海德就在他面前，当场用药粉调配了一剂滋滋作响的药水。就在海德把药剂拿到嘴边准备喝下时，他转过头来对蓝扬说：“你应该p.38还记得我们决定当医生之时所做的宣誓吧，我亲爱的蓝扬。”

这个男人的熟悉感让蓝扬大为惊讶。

“接下来发生的事，”海德继续说，完全不管另一个人的感觉，“就当作是我们两人的秘密。”他把药剂一饮而尽，然后一阵摇摇晃晃地，他赶紧往前倾靠在柜子上以免跌倒。

几乎就在喝下药剂的同时，他身体上的转变就开始了。

满脸横肉的爱德华·海德，缓慢而显著地转变成高尚文雅的亨利·杰科尔。

p.39 “老天，这是怎么回事？”蓝扬惊叫。

“老天跟今晚这件事无关。”海德用低哑的声音答道，但他的声音已渐渐变得柔和，不那么粗声粗气了。

等到这个过程终于结束，现在已完全变回杰科尔的这个人站在柜子旁，蓝扬走过去扶着他朋友的手臂，“这到底是怎么……”

杰科尔摇摇头，“今天的事，请你千万不要对外人说。”他说道，声音略微提高。

p.40 “你应该去找人帮忙。”话未说完，他的朋友已经消失在黑夜中了。

“把抽屉送回去，亲爱的蓝扬。”杰科尔毫无生气的声音，从渺渺茫茫的浓雾中传出来。

几个星期过后，普尔去拜访阿特森，他请求这位律师立刻随他前往主人的宅邸，因为他主人竟然把自己锁在实验室里。

他们两个人刻不容缓，快步穿越城镇，向杰科尔的屋子奔去，在路上，普尔上气不接下气地对阿特森说：“他已经在里面好几天了。”

“还有，”普尔透露，“我从实验室外面听到的声音，让我越来越担心了。”

“你听到什么声音了，亲爱的管家？”

“他的声音，先生，完全不像我家主人的声音。”

p.41 到了杰科尔家中，当管家在实验室外不断地敲着门，从里面传出的回应声很显然地完全不同了，变得粗糙、嘶哑。“我什么人都不想见。”这个声音回答道。

“我怀疑我的主人被魔鬼附身了。”普尔低声说道。

“你说他已经在里面好几天了？”

普尔点点头，“真正算起来有八天了，又哭又叫的像是精神失常的人。同时他又派我到处去送信，送给所有我认识的药剂师，以及我根本不认识的药剂师。”

p.42 “信上都写些什么？”

“都是要买一些药剂或药物。每次我把东西带回来后，总是又写了一封信要我拿去退还，因为药物不纯，然后又要我到别家公司去买。他很迫切需要这些药，不知是什么原因。”

“你手边有没有留下这些信？”

管家蹙着眉，拍拍口袋，然后伸手进去摸到一张皱成一团的纸条，他把纸条摊平之后，拿给阿特森。

“你主人要的药，那个药剂师都能调配出来？”阿特森看着纸条时问。

普尔懊恼地摇着头，“才不呢，药剂师告诉我，博士要的那种药已经停止生产了，显然他自己之前买了最后一批。所以我只能空手而回，就在这个时候……”管家停顿下来，望了一眼关着的门，“就在这个时候，里p.43面的那个人——我不认为那个人是我主人——就勃然大怒。”

“你不必担心，普尔，这确实是博士的笔迹。”

普尔急切地点头。“是的，阿特森先生，”他最后说，“是博士的笔迹没错，或者至少模仿得非常像。但是，笔迹算什么？我见过他本人了。”

“见过他本人？”

“是的，先生。我看到的时间前后不到一分钟，但是已足以让我毛骨悚然了。先生，如果他是我的主人，为何在看到我的时候，会大惊失色，还落荒而逃？”

“是海德先生吗？”

“是的，先生，”普尔非常肯定地说。“我相信是他没错。”

阿特森评估之后，认定唯一能做的，就是破门而入了。于是他差派仆役守住另一个通道，吩咐他不准让任p.44何人通过。然后，他们带着斧头和拨火棒，回到门口。

“杰科尔，”阿特森大喊，“我要见你。”他停了一下，但是里面没有回音。“我警告你，我们已对你产生怀疑了，我非见到你不可，如果你不让我们进来，那我们只好破门而入。”

“阿特森，”里面传来嘶吼声，“拜托你行行好。”

“这绝非我朋友的声音，”阿特森轻声对管家说。“是海德的声音。撞门，普尔！”

普尔持续用斧头猛击，不到几分钟，厚重的大门就被破坏了，阿特森立刻冲入屋内，而屋子里似乎一片寂静。炉床上的火正噼里啪啦地烧着，抽屉都被打开了，里面的物品一目了然，但排得整整齐齐的。而在火炉边，喝茶的器具都摆得好好的，茶壶也在火炉上咕嘟咕嘟地滚煮着。

然而，在地板中央躺着一个人，并且

还在抽搐着。

p.45 阿特森弯下身子，将这个人翻过身来，这个人就是爱德华·海德，只是他身上的衣服对他而言，实在太大了。“我们恐怕来迟了，”阿特森抓起海德的手腕，摸了摸他的脉搏说，“接下来我们该做的，就是去找你主人的尸体了。”

p.46 经过一场大规模的搜寻之后，阿特森和普尔都没有找到杰科尔博士的踪迹，不管是生或死。

“先生，这里有一封信。”普尔从长桌上大声呼喊着，“指名要给你的。”

阿特森走向管家，打开信封。“什么？这是杰科尔的遗嘱，”阿特森说，“他重新拟了一份，原来受益人写海德的地方，你的主人全都改成我的名字了。”阿特森将注意力转回长桌，又发现了另一封信件。这封信注明了日期，里面有两封信件——一封是杰科尔本人写的，另一封是蓝扬医生写的。

“当天杰科尔一定在场，”阿特森说。“他不可能在这么短的时间内被杀，然后还被埋葬好。他一定是逃走了，但他为什么要逃呢？”

“或许答案就在这两封信里。”普尔大胆地猜测。

p.47 律师点点头，“或许，但我可以预见，你的主人已经遭遇某种可怕的灾厄了。”

在天色未亮之前，阿特森已经得知他朋友所有的愚蠢行为。他读完了蓝扬所述在年初看到海德不可思议的变身过程；也读了杰科尔自己沉痛地坦陈想要提升医学知识的决心，完全不考虑自己的安全或健康。他也读了亨利·杰科尔谈到他的信念，他认为人的实体不是一个，而是两个，就好像一个铜板的两面，一个是善，一个是恶。“如果善与恶两种本质，”杰科尔写道，“能够以两种不同的身份独立存在，那么人生便能从难以忍受的桎梏中得到解放。”

阿特森读到最后，绝望地抱着头。天啊，他的朋友

p.48 发现了每一个人都必定包容他完整的自我，包括同时存在于同一个身份与身体内的善与恶。真正让生命难以承受的原因，是没有办法去平衡同一身份和同一个身体里的两股相反的力量。

后 记

改编版

改编版的《化身博士》，是由罗伯特·路易斯·史蒂文森伟大且恐怖的短篇小说改写而成。如果你想阅读完整的原版小说，领略原著的光彩，市面上有很多完整的版本贩售，从廉价的平装书，到装帧精致的精装书都有。在当地图书馆或慈善义卖商店也可以找得到。

原貌重现

在精简小说的过程中，有很多史蒂文森的原文词句都被删除了，虽然可惜但却又不得不为。虽然不多，但我们也做出了一些艰难的取舍，省略了次要情节。下列要点可以帮助你从精简版的《化身博士》，进入史蒂文森的原著堂奥。

- 阿特森对于他朋友要修改遗嘱这件事很担心，由于他试图了解杰科尔的动机，因此展开了探索的过程，最后才发现博士的愚行。

- 当阿特森第一次遇到海德时，他觉得海德的长相不仅畸形丑陋，甚至还像个穴居人——穴居人是指终日生活在地底下不见天日的人。

- 阿特森相信，杰科尔一定犯了什么不可对人言的罪行，而海德知道内情。

- 当他去找杰科尔询问时，杰科尔解释他跟海德的关系是“说了也解决不了的那种关系”，这暗示了其实杰科尔在故事刚开始不久，就意识到自己很可能会失去控制。

- 在原著里，杀害丹佛·卡鲁爵士的那一段叙述是非常残忍的：“这位年迈的绅士受了些伤，神情相当惊讶地往后退了一步；海德先生毫不留情地用手杖将他打倒在地。接着，他像只发狂的猩猩，把这个受害者踩在脚下，使劲地践踏，力道之强，都可以听到底下这个人骨头碎掉的声音。”

- 当纽卡曼警官陪同阿特森一起前往海德的房间视察时，他们发现了很多双重人格的迹象：“有个摆满酒的柜子，盘子是银制的，还有雅致的餐巾，墙上还挂了一幅挺有水准的画。”“但是衣服却一堆一堆地四处乱丢，仿佛这个地方刚被洗劫过一样。”

- 在故事结束之前，蓝扬博士染上了急症，不久就去世了。阿特森在他朋友死后，收到了蓝扬指名寄给他的信，还附加了一个条件：“假如他先死，这封信就不拆封直接销毁。”

● 我们是在亨利·杰科尔用自己的话所写的最后一封信里，了解他亲身经历的恐怖经验。

历史回顾

罗伯特·路易斯·史蒂文森是在 1886 年，也就是他36岁的时候，完成了《化身博士》这部作品。在当时，他已经以冒险小说和奇幻故事这类型的有趣小说享誉盛名。例如《金银岛》，这是描写惊险刺激的寻宝故事。但他最吸引人的作品，当然同时也造成一时洛阳纸贵的作品，正是《化身博士》。在短短的几个月内，这本书就卖了四万本；而到了20世纪，累计已卖出至少25万本。

史蒂文森一直对人性中的善恶两面很感兴趣。他活在一个强烈注重礼节、名声以及合宜举止的社会里，而这样的文明行为，往往会导致人们压抑他们性格中的其他部分，例如情欲、肉体，以及愤怒。

此时的英国，正值探索及征服新世界之时，而在那些新世界的文化里，他们的行为举止多与维多利亚时期的英国人大不相同，并且通常会被贴上“野蛮人”的标签。当时的英国人虽然会害怕这些“野蛮人”，但同时又深受吸引，或许是因为他们发现，自己的内在也有同样的野蛮倾向。

在19世纪时期，伦敦很多地区都变得拥挤又肮脏，因此，贫穷和疾病都是可怕的社会问题。像杰科尔这种阶层的人，或许会选择视若无睹，但他们不可能不会察觉到，在他们中间存在着许多“较不文明”的人。史蒂文森想要去探索——以杰科尔博士的话来说——“人类，其实并不是只有一个实体，而是两个。”

维多利亚女王统治时期，在科学、技术和医学方面，都有长足的进展。在 1886 年，麻醉剂和防腐剂已广为使用，而且人们对于科学的潜在力量兴趣日增，也因此进行了不少科学实验。这提供了史帝文森撰写这个故事的医学背景。

史蒂文森一找到描写双重人格的切入点之后，他下笔如神，速度快到或许不到三天就写完了整本书。

延伸思考

如果你是一个人读这本《化身博士》，这里列出了一些可供思考的重点；你若是和朋友一起阅读，这里也提供了一些值得讨论的观点。

在重新改写这个故事时，我们试着重新创造出尽可能忠于原著的情节与人物。我们同时也试着模仿他的写作风格。但请记住，无论如何，本书并非原著，因此，思考下列要点，只能帮你一窥史蒂文森写作技巧之堂奥。请从此处出发，再进入完整原著，让自己沉浸在作者精彩绝伦的叙事魔力之中。

思考发想

- 作者经常使用城市本身来当作一个角色，以营造气氛。请从书中找出这样的例子。

- 你认为阿特森是乐于助人的角色吗？还是你认为他很爱管闲事？

- 你认为为何史蒂文森的书里，都没有女性的角色？你如何看待这些主要角色中没有人在谈情说爱？

- 你认为海德的哪些方面是和他相遇的人最为关注的？

故事主题

你觉得罗伯特·路易斯·史蒂文森针对以下主题，有什么看法？

- 人性的善恶两面

- 文明社会与人类

- 科学实验

- 友谊与诚实

写作风格

你能够在书中找出有关以下范例的段落吗？

- 感叹号的使用
- 景色的描写
- 用短句来制造悬疑紧张的气氛
- 使用老式语言的句子

仔细观察这些文章段落是如何写出来的。你注意到什么了吗？你可以用相同的风格写出一段文字吗？

FINDING OUT MORE

英文延伸阅读

我们推荐以下书目及网站，帮助读者更加了解罗伯特·路易斯·史蒂文森，以及他所生活的世界。

书目

- Jenni Calder, *RLS: A Life Study*, Hamilton, 1980.
- Edwin M. Eigner, *Robert Louis Stevenson and Romantic Tradition*, Princeton University Press, 1966.
- Ann Kramer, *Victorians* (Eyewitness Guides), Dorling Kindersley, 1998.
- Terry Deary, *Vile Victorians* (Horrible Histories), Scholastic, 1994.
- Natasha Narayan, *The Timetraveller's Guide to Victorian London*, Timetraveller's Guides, 2004.

网站

- http://dinamico.unibg.it/rls/rls.htm

  你可以找到各种有关史蒂文森的相关资讯。

- http://www.gradesaver.com/classicnotes/titles/jekyll/themes.html

  本站针对杰科尔的两种身份，以及伦敦的双重城市角色，做了比较；也就是一个是阴郁、压抑，另一个是开放、热闹。

- http://www.bbc.co.uk/history/british/victorians

  这是英国国家广播电台有关英国维多利亚时期的互动网站，提供了广泛的资讯，以及适合各年龄层的活动。

- http://www.gradesaver.com/classicnotes/quiz/jekyll/I/

  此网站有免费的测验，你试试看能答对多少题。

电影

- 《变身怪医》（1931）米高梅出品。鲁本·马莫利安执导
- 《化身博士》（1981）英国国家广播电台 / Second Sight 出品。阿拉斯塔尔·雷德执导。
- 《化身博士摇滚音乐剧》（2002），安德烈·香槟执导。
- 《化身博士》（2006）影像娱乐公司出品，约翰·卡尔·布奇勒执导。
- 《化身博士杰科尔》（2007）英国国家广播电台 / Contender 出品。这是电视版的《化身博士》，内容描写杰科尔的后代，生活在当今时代的虚构故事。